St. Hans' Evening Play Overture

Recent Researches in Music

A-R Editions publishes seven series of critical editions, spanning the history of Western music, American music, and oral traditions.

Recent Researches in the Music of the Middle Ages and Early Renaissance
    Charles M. Atkinson, general editor

Recent Researches in the Music of the Renaissance
    James Haar, general editor

Recent Researches in the Music of the Baroque Era
    Christoph Wolff, general editor

Recent Researches in the Music of the Classical Era
    Eugene K. Wolf, general editor

Recent Researches in the Music of the Nineteenth and Early Twentieth Centuries
    Rufus Hallmark, general editor

Recent Researches in American Music
    John M. Graziano, general editor

Recent Researches in the Oral Traditions of Music
    Philip V. Bohlman, general editor

Each edition in *Recent Researches* is devoted to works by a single composer or to a single genre. The content is chosen for its high quality and historical importance, and each edition includes a substantial introduction and critical report. The music is engraved according to the highest standards of production using the proprietary software MusE, owned by MusicNotes, Inc.

For information on establishing a standing order to any of our series, or for editorial guidelines on submitting proposals, please contact:

A-R Editions, Inc.
Middleton, Wisconsin

800 736-0070 (U.S. book orders)
608 836-9000 (phone)
608 831-8200 (fax)
http://www.areditions.com

Recent Researches in the Music of the Nineteenth and Early Twentieth Centuries, 32

Niels W. Gade

St. Hans' Evening Play Overture

Edited by Anna Harwell Celenza

A-R Editions, Inc.
Middleton, Wisconsin

To James Haar and R. Larry Todd

A-R Editions, Inc., Middleton, Wisconsin
© 2001 by A-R Editions, Inc.

All rights reserved. No part of this edition may be reproduced or transmitted in any form by any electronic or mechanical means (including photocopying, recording, or information storage and retrieval) without permission in writing from the publisher.

The purchase of this edition does not convey the right to perform it in public, nor to make a recording of it for any purpose. Such permission must be obtained in advance from the publisher.

A-R Editions is pleased to support scholars and performers in their use of *Recent Researches* material for study or performance. Subscribers to any of the *Recent Researches* series, as well as patrons of subscribing institutions, are invited to apply for information about our "Copyright Sharing Policy."

Printed in the United States of America

ISBN 0-89579-480-2
ISSN 0193-5364

∞ The paper used in this publication meets the minimum requirements of the American National Standard for Information Sciences—Permanence of Paper for Printed Library Materials, ANSI Z39.48-1984.

Contents

Acknowledgments vi

Introduction vii

  Adam Oehlenschläger's *St. Hans' Evening Play* vii
  Niels W. Gade's *St. Hans' Evening Play Overture* viii
  Notes xiii

Plates xvi

St. Hans' Evening Play Overture 1

Critical Report 103

  Sources 103
  Editorial Methods 103
  Critical Notes 103

Acknowledgments

This edition benefited greatly from the time and effort of many friends and colleagues, and I would like to thank especially those who helped me see it to completion. To Niels Martin Jensen, I offer "mange tak" for his encouragement and invaluable guidance. Also deserving thanks are Niels Bo Foltmann, Finn Egeland Hansen, Anne Ørbaek Jensen, Claus Røllum-Larsen, and Niels Krabbe. Thanks to the Royal Library in Copenhagen for allowing me to reproduce items from their collection, and thanks to the Fulbright Foundation, the Dronning Margrethe og Prins Henrik Fond (Denmark), and the Idella Foundation (Liechtenstein) for their financial support. Finally, thanks to my husband, Christopher S. Celenza, for his many years of love and encouragement.

Introduction

On 30 March 1841 Niels W. Gade (1817–90) enjoyed a stunning success when his concert overture, *Echoes of Ossian*, won first prize in a competition sponsored by the Copenhagen Music Society. Bearing the motto "Formel hält Uns nicht Gebunden, unsere Kunst heißt Poesie,"[1] this composition represented Gade's first successful completion of a large-scale orchestral work and the beginning of a brilliant career.

After winning the Music Society's competition, Gade began working on a piano arrangement of his overture for publication.[2] In a letter to Carl Helsted dated 28 July 1841, Gade related, with great relief, the completion of this tedious project, and then described his newest musical undertaking:

> I have begun an overture to Oehlenschläger's *St. Hans' Evening Play* which will be in a light and more cheerful tone; except for that I haven't done anything this summer.[3]

Turning to Gade's composition diary, we see that he worked on the overture throughout the month of August and finished it in September 1841.[4] According to Gade, the overture was "based on Oehlenschläger's *St. Hans' Evening Play*."[5] Therefore we should acquaint ourselves with the play itself before examining Gade's music.

Adam Oehlenschläger's *St. Hans' Evening Play*

Written in one long act with a prologue and epilogue, Oehlenschläger's *St. Hans' Evening Play* combines a wide variety of poetic forms, moods, and perspectives in a richly textured portrayal of contemporary bourgeois society.[6] Intending to capture, as had Shakespeare,[7] the magical atmosphere of Midsummer Night (i.e., St. Hans' Evening in Denmark[8]), Oehlenschläger sets his play in Copenhagen's Dyrehave (Deer Park)[9] and alternates scenes of a raucous midsummer carnival and enchanted forest with episodes from the touching love-story of Ludvig and Maria.

The prologue opens with a speech by an old vagabond. Acting as the prologus he climbs an ancient burial mound and greets the audience:

> Welcome to the red hour of daybreak,
> each of you who now has gathered here
> to follow us—with persevering, healthy feet—
> from the sluggish fog of the city to
> yonder forest, which arches green and cool . . .[10]

In awe of nature's beauty, the vagabond then breaks into a rhapsodical morning song. At the song's conclusion Harlequin appears.[11] Claiming to be "the genuine prologus," he dismisses the vagabond and then continues, much in the style of a *Märchenkomodie*, by insulting the audience and taking stabs at figures such as Shakespeare, Homer, and various drama critics.[12] Toward the end of Harlequin's speech, the rural setting for the prologue is transformed into the living room of a middle-class, urban home, and the audience is prepared for the commencement of the play:

> Now we have all been dragged to the city.
> Yet the unity of the play has not been observed exactly;
> thus those who are not partial to change
> can stay behind when we next rearrange.
> We are now in the home of a common man.
> None other than Hillemænd! See, he is approaching.
> It would be best for me to yield to this person;
> I do not want to spoil the illusion.[13]

The home belongs to Maria's foster parents; the man approaching is her foster father. He tells the audience her tragic story: Maria has fallen in love with a handsome young count named Ludvig, but her mother feels the relationship is futile, for he is "well above her station." So the poor girl has been sent away so that time and distance will lessen her distress. Naturally, just the opposite has happened: time has only increased her love for Ludvig, and their separation has caused her great sorrow. In an effort to lift the young girl's spirits, her foster parents decide to take her to the Dyrehave. Maria is comforted by the idea of escaping the city. While her foster parents prepare for the journey, she enlists the help of a servant girl and plans a secret rendezvous with Ludvig.

A brief lyric interlude, "De Kiørende" (The Driving Ones), provides the transition from the city to the country, and the travelers soon arrive at the carnival-like setting of the Dyrehave, where Maria's foster father meets a "young man from Langeland." Unaware that the lad is in fact Ludvig, he introduces him to Maria and his wife, and the four spend the day together. They visit several attractions, including a glass-blower, puppet show, pantomimes, exotic animals, tight-rope walker, dog act, and a public drinking house. At the close of the scene the crowd thins as evening approaches.

A second lyric passage, "Gyngesang" (Swing Song), transports the audience deeper into the forest, and

Ludvig and Maria again become the focus of attention. As the night scene opens, Ludvig sits alone and sings a lament while Maria slowly makes her way toward him. Finally the lovers are reunited—the fantasy begins as Maria sings a hymn that resounds through the forest:

> Magical Harmony
> in earth's midnight darkness!
> Blessed Sympathy!
> Holy Poetry
> without words!
> Amalgamation of grove and sea
> and stars, and a youth and maiden locked in an embrace!
> Arm in arm
> the whole of Nature interprets the name of Love.[14]

The forest takes on magical overtones: an ancient oak tree and a tiny glow-worm (St. Hans' worm) compare life experiences, Death frolics through the trees singing a macabre song, and St. Kirsten approaches her sacred spring and, much to the delight of the personified waves, sheds fresh tears.[15] Throughout these fantastic happenings Maria and Ludvig remain entwined in one another's arms. At midnight, however, they are awakened from their dream by the chimes of a distant clock tower. They realize that their reunion can only be temporary. But just as they are about to depart, "The Genie of Love" appears and tells them of an enchanted place where they can escape. Without a word, the lovers abandon their responsibilities and retire to the blissful retreat.

At the play's conclusion a hunter wanders through the forest and delivers an epilogue about universal love and nature. He then blows his horn and departs, leaving a flock of small birds behind to sing the closing chorus:

> In the moonlight
> behind a latticework of branches
> we birds so small
> peep at each other and sing:
> Thank God, we are united
> on our small little branch!
> Only when it is safe
> for us to hop around free,
> oh, then we are so happy,
> so happy, so happy!
> Kweereeleet, Kweereeleet![16]

Niels W. Gade's *St. Hans' Evening Play* Overture

Turning to Gade's overture, we readily recognize several scenes from Oehlenschläger's play. Gade begins his composition with a morning scene. Whereas Oehlenschläger describes "the red hour of daybreak" through the words of his vagabond prologus, Gade uses the arpeggiated melody of a solo horn (see example 1a) for the same purpose in his slow introduction. An echo of the horn is heard in measure 22,[17] and in measure 25 the bassoon and violins repeat the arpeggiated theme—again followed by a horn echo in measure 34. The dawn of a new day is further characterized by a gradual thickening of the texture and twittering bird calls played by the flute (mm. 38–44).

A transition marked *stringendo poco a poco* begins in measure 51 at rehearsal letter A (example 1b). Foreshadowing the arrival of the primary theme, this section grows in dynamics and rushes headlong until, in an explosion of rhythmic activity, it yields to the *Allegro con viverra* in measure 71. Here we meet the exposition's vibrant primary theme. This theme, played in unison by the upper strings and woodwinds and accompanied by full and arpeggiated chords in the brass, lower strings, and bassoon, depicts the carnival-like setting of Oehlenschläger's Dyrehave (example 1c).

At the end of the primary theme, a second transition section appears (mm. 93–123, rehearsal letter B). Depicting the forest setting from Oehlenschläger's play, the first nineteen measures of this section are characterized by rippling eighth-note passages in the strings (St. Kirsten's spring), a tranquil neighbor-note motive in the third horn, and bird calls in the upper woodwinds (example 1d). Toward the end of this section (m. 112) the carnivalesque primary theme returns; but like the crowd of revelers in Oehlenschläger's Dyrehave, the texture of this section thins (m. 120) and the theme fades away (mm. 121–23).

The secondary theme begins in measure 124 (rehearsal letter C). Soaring above the gentle, syncopated accompaniment of the strings (marked "dolce"), this E-major melody reflects the interminable love of Ludvig and Maria (example 1e). As in his previous overtures (e.g., *Agnete and the Merman* and *Echoes of Ossian*), Gade chose an upper-woodwind instrument to play this stirring love theme.[18] Occasional chromatic tones in the strings (for example, mm. 132–33 and 137–40) add a certain poignancy to the music, recalling Maria's impassioned hymn during the climax of the play: "Magical Harmony in earth's midnight darkness! Blessed Sympathy! Holy Poetry without words!" A repetition of the secondary theme begins in measure 156; this version of the theme contains running eighth-note passages similar to those in the carnival music of the primary theme (mm. 156–69, first violins).

In the opening of the development (m. 170, rehearsal letter D), motives from the previous two transitions are presented simultaneously: the strings play the characteristic rhythmic motive first encountered in the *stringendo poco a poco* section (mm. 51–70), while the horn and upper woodwinds repeat the tranquil neighbor-note motive and bird calls from the forest scene in measures 93–123. These motives are soon joined by an echo of the secondary theme in the clarinet and cello (mm. 173–78). A treatment of the primary theme dominates the development from measure 186 and progresses through several modulations: E major (mm. 170–84), A minor (mm. 185–94), C major (mm. 195–206). Variants of the secondary theme in the key of E major return in measure 207 but soon yield to a return of the primary theme in C major (m. 227, rehearsal letter E). Further harmonic development includes modulations to A minor (m. 239), G major (m. 245), C minor (m. 251), C major (m. 260), and E major (m. 272).

Example 1

a) Prologus' morning song / Epilogus' hunting horn (mm. 3–6)

b) Transition to Dyrehave (De Kiørende) (mm. 54–57)

c) Carnival at Dyrehave (primary theme) (mm. 71–72)

d) The enchanted forest (mm. 96–98)

e) Love theme of Ludvig and Maria (secondary theme) (mm. 124–29)

Toward the end of the development an animated transition similar to measures 51–71 leads to the recapitulation. Here Gade takes special care to avoid merely retracing the thematic course of the exposition. A return of the forest music in the tonic key prepares the way for a final presentation of the primary theme (m. 304). Ludvig's and Maria's love theme returns in measure 336 and after several repetitions closes with a slight ritard leading to the coda. Marked *tempo primo,* the coda features a return of the horn melody from the slow introduction. The return of this theme is significant; in addition to supplying the work with a sense of thematic closure, it refers to the horn call played by the hunter in the epilogue of Oehlenschläger's play. The overture concludes with a faint echo of the midsummer carnival in the key of F major (mm. 434–39, violins) and a hint of Ludwig's and Maria's love theme (mm. 442–46, oboe). A plagal cadence announces the overture's final resolution.

The earliest sketches for *St. Hans' Evening Play*[19] confirm that, from the beginning, Gade intended to use the intricate complex of thematic ideas found in the final version. Written in piano reduction with full details of scoring and dynamics, these sketches present almost exactly the overture's final form. Except for the omission of several minor repetitive passages, the only revisions involve a slight remodeling of the secondary theme. In the sketches this theme is symmetrical and more folk-like in character. In fact, it appears that an actual folk tune, melody 48B of *Udvalgte danske Viser,* may have served as the theme's original model (see example 2).

Example 2
a) Original secondary theme

b) Folk tune #48B from *Udvalgte danske Viser*

But Gade did not draw on folk music alone. His primary musical models for *St. Hans' Evening Play* appear to have been Mendelssohn's *The Fair Melusine* (1833) and *A Midsummer Night's Dream* (1826) overtures. Gade was well acquainted with *The Fair Melusine*,[20] and it appears that the overture's lyricism and sanguine opening influenced the creation of *St. Hans' Evening Play*. But these are only superficial similarities. In terms of thematic structure and form Gade's primary model was Mendelssohn's *A Midsummer Night's Dream*. Although this overture was not premiered in Copenhagen until 1843,[21] parts of it were used in 1835 as a prelude to the Royal Theater's productions of J. L. Heiberg's *Alferne*.[22] No great leap of faith is needed to imagine that the young Gade somehow gained access to the score, since as a member of the Royal Chapel he played violin in the theater orchestra from 1834 to 1838.

In addition to a similarity in programs (the magical happenings of midsummer night), *St. Hans' Evening Play* and *A Midsummer Night's Dream* display a similar approach to thematic content, motivic development, and formal construction. In his most recent discussion of *A Midsummer Night's Dream*, R. Larry Todd draws attention to the "especially rich thematic content" displayed in the overture. "Animated by no fewer than six sharply delineated figures," the exposition presents the listener with an array of dramatic scenes and characters.[23] Impressed by Mendelssohn's use of distinctive themes as a means of relating the various dramatic parts of a program, Gade adopted a similar procedure in the *St. Hans' Evening Play* overture. Like *A Midsummer Night's Dream*, this work's exposition contains several themes representing scenes and characters from the play (example 1).

As Todd explains, although each of Mendelssohn's six motives enjoys its own special character, they are all the product of a series of metamorphoses that traces its development from a common source—the four wind chords of the overture's opening motto.[24] Gade used a similar method of motivic transformation in the various themes for *St. Hans' Evening Play*. Whereas Mendelssohn concealed the motivic germ of his overture in its opening chords, Gade chose to present it prominently in his overture's initial horn call (example 1a). Outlining a major triad, this melody generates the basic building block for the overture's subsequent thematic ideas. The themes in examples 1b and 1c frame the triad in their leaps and scalar passages, and example 1e plainly displays a triad in the love theme of Ludvig and Maria. At first glance example 1d might appear free from the influence of this device, but close inspection of the accompaniment reveals a triadic structure in the strings and bassoon. Even the general harmonic structure of the overture is affected by the triad: its principal tonal areas—tonic, mediant, and dominant—reflect a major/minor triad (table 1).

In the formal plan of *St. Hans' Evening Play* Gade avoided a routine, sequential ordering of the various thematic elements in the development and recapitulation.[25] By mixing the diverse thematic ideas and varying their order of appearance, Gade succeeded in his attempt to create an intricate and subtle composition (table 2).

When Gade completed *St. Hans' Evening Play* in September 1841, he was quite pleased with the work. In a letter to Carl Helsted dated 15 October he wrote:

Dear Brother and Friend!
. . . After a fraternal greeting and salute I hereby inform you that I find myself in the best of health, fresh as a fish. . . . I have written a new ditto to Oehlenschläger's *St. Hans' Evening Play* in A major that I will have performed at a concert in the Theater. Very merry and also erotic (a pretty piece).[26]

The performance mentioned above was none other than Clara Schumann's first concert at Copenhagen's Royal Theater (3 April 1842).[27] In a letter to her husband Clara commented on Gade's overture:

At my concert Gade will present a new overture that is quite different from the first; it is completely cheerful in character.[28]

In addition to Clara's approving words, Gade's overture received glowing reviews from the press. A critic for the paper *Fædrelandet* wrote:

TABLE 1
General harmonic structure of *St. Hans' Evening Play Overture*

Section	Key		Measure
Introduction	A major	A (I)	1
Exposition (primary theme)		A (I)	51
(secondary theme)		E (V)	124
Development		E (V)	170
		a (i)	185
		C (III)	195
		E (V)	207
		C (III)	227
	A minor	a (i)	239
		G (VII [V/iii])	245
		c (iii)	251
		C (III)	260
		E (V)	272
Recapitulation	A major	A (I)	288
(primary theme)		A (I)	304
(secondary theme)		A (I)	336
Coda		A (I)	400
(primary theme: echo)		F (♭VI)	434
		A (I)	439

TABLE 2
Thematic structure of *St. Hans' Evening Play Overture*

	Introduction	Exposition						
Theme (example 1):	a	b	c	d	(c)	(b)	e	(c)
Key:	A						E	
Measure:	1	51	71	93	112	116	124	156

	Development															
	d(b)	(e)	b	(c)	c	b	(e)	e	d	(b)	c					b
	E		a		C			E			C	a	G	c	C	E
	170	174	185	187	195	199	201	207	215	224	227					275

	Recapitulation					Coda			
	d	c	(a)	e	(d)	a(e)		c	e
	A							F	A
	288	104	330	336	368	400		434	441	448

Last evening the public was given the opportunity to enjoy a new work by the talented, young composer, Herr Gade—an overture to Oehlenschläger's *St. Hans' Evening Play*. Like his previous [overture], this composition distinguished itself by beautiful ideas, originality in treatment, and a prizeworthy detachment from all pursuits after external effects. The composer received a warm and honorable recognition from all those knowledgeable in music.[29]

A similar review appeared in another Copenhagen paper, *Det Berlingske Tidene*:

Among the other numbers on the concert we especially must emphasize our talented *Capelmusicus* N.W. Gade's new overture to Oehlenschläger's *St. Hans' Evening Play*, which was received with lively applause.[30]

When Gade first presented his overture to the Royal Theater in 1841, its cover page contained the following inscription (see plate 1):

Overture to Oehlenschläger's "St. Hans' Evening Play"
(op. ?) (September 1841)[31]

As the opus marking on the title page reveals, Gade originally intended to publish the overture, but his plans never came to fruition. Despite the positive reviews from Clara Schumann and Copenhagen's critics, Gade's St.

Hans' Evening Play was never performed outside Denmark. This might seem strange at first, given the international attention received by Gade's *Echoes of Ossian* overture just one year before. But a brief investigation of Danish and German publishing practices reveals that the overture's failed publication was likely due to its distinctly Danish program.

During the first half of the nineteenth century, music publishers in Denmark and Germany tended to print compositions that would appeal to an international, amateur market. Chamber music was favored, especially works for keyboard, flute, and/or violin.[32] Orchestral works were published less often due to expensive production costs, though keyboard arrangements of these works had a better chance at publication if they carried titles and/or programs familiar to a large portion of the consumer population. Simply stated, composers in Denmark had to write music for an international market if they hoped to get published. And Oehlenschläger's *St. Hans' Evening Play* was not familiar to readers outside Scandinavia.

Oehlenschläger's *St. Hans' Evening Play* was hailed as a literary milestone in Denmark,[33] but it failed to gain international acclaim. Although the majority of Oehlenschläger's works were translated and published by foreign publishers shortly after their appearance in Denmark, such was not the case with *St. Hans' Evening Play*.[34] Consequently, music publishers found little hope for financial profit in Gade's overture. The limited consumer market of Oehlenschläger's play, combined with the expense of printing an orchestral work, dissuaded publishers from investing in Gade's overture.

After the 1842 premiere and failed attempt at publication, Gade set *St. Hans' Evening Play* aside and did not return to it until sometime during the 1860s, when he made an inventory of his manuscripts and sketches. We can tell from comments added to the title page that Gade was uncertain about what he should do with the manuscript:

> Overture to Oehlenschläger's "St. Hans' Evening Play"
> (op. ?) (September 1841)
> Cast out (?)
> Must be "reworked."[35]

He considered throwing the manuscript out, but on second thought decided to keep it and return to it in the future.

Gade began revising *St. Hans' Evening Play* in the summer of 1870. At this time he returned to the original 1841 score and entered various changes. Gade's musical corrections are detailed in the critical notes, but his most dramatic revision appeared on the score's title page (plate 1). In an attempt to make the overture more accessible to non-Danish audiences, Gade veiled the original connection to Oehlenschläger's play by changing the title of his overture to *A Summer Day Love-Idyll*:

> <u>Originally Overture</u> to Oehlenschläger's "St. Hans' Evening Play"
> (op. ?) (September <u>1841</u>)
> Cast out (?)
> Must be "reworked."
> A Summer Day
> Love-Idyll Overture (1870)[36]

Unfortunately, no fair copy of *A Summer Day Love-Idyll* exists. Thus we can only assume that Gade abandoned this project shortly after its undertaking in the summer of 1870.[37]

Notes

1. This motto comes from a popular poem entitled "Freie Kunst" by the German poet Ludwig Uhland.

2. In a letter to Edvard Collin dated 12 April 1841 (Royal Library: Collin Saml. nr. 314), Gade states that he has begun working on the four-hand piano arrangement of the overture.

3. William Behrend, "Omkring Niels W. Gade," *Aarbog for Musik* (1922/23): 65–66. The original letter is in the Helsted family's private collection. "Jeg har begyndt paa en Ouv: til St. Hansaften-Spil af Øhlenschläger som skal være i en let og heater Tone, Firestone har jeg ikke bestilt noget I Sommer." The translations used throughout this essay are all my own.

4. Written between July 1839 and September 1841, this diary contains the programmatic origins for seven of Gade's early compositions: the published *Echoes of Ossian* overture (Op. 1); C-minor Symphony (Op. 5); Piano Sonata in E minor (Op. 28); and *Agnete and the Merman* (Op. 3); and the unpublished Trio in B-flat major for Violin, Cello, and Piano; String Quartet in F major; and *St. Hans' Evening Play* overture. Gade's diary was given to Det kongelige Bibliotek shortly after his death, but it is now lost. Photocopies of the original, however, still exist. I would like to thank Niels Martin Jensen for allowing me to consult his copy of the original. A complete transcription and translation of the diary is included in my book, *The Early Works of Niels W. Gade: In Search of the Poetic* (Aldershot: Ashgate, 2001) and in my dissertation (published under the name Harwell), " 'Unsre Kunst Heißt Poesie': Niels W. Gade's Early Compositions and Their Programmatic Origins" (Ph.D. diss., Duke University, 1996), 267–74.

5. "efter 'St. Hansaftenspil' af Øhlenschläger."

6. The immediate model for Oehlenschläger's *St. Hans' Evening Play* was Goethe's youthful shrovetide farce, *Das Jahrmarktsfest zu Plundersweilern* (see Wilhelm Dietrich Lippstadt, *Oehlenschlägers "Sankt Hansaftenspil" im Abhängigkeitsverhältnis zur deutschen Literatur* [Borna-Leipzig, 1916]). Yet as Kathryn Shailer Hansen, "Adam Oehlenschläger and Ludwig Tieck: A Study in Danish and German Romanticism" (Ph.D. diss., Princeton University, 1978), 78–79, explains, although "both evoke a bustling carnival atmosphere and make use of similar stock characters, in terms of actual setting, scope and purpose, the two bear little relationship."

7. Oehlenschläger was quite familiar with Shakespeare's play; he published a Danish translation of the work entitled *En*

Skiærsommernats Drøm. Lystspil af Shakespeare. Oversat af Adam Oehlenschläger (Copenhagen: Brünnich paa Oversætternes Forlag, 1816).

8. Rooted in the traditions of pre-Christian Denmark, St. Han's Evening (June 23) marks Denmark's observance of the summer solstice. According to popular legend, the powers of nature are especially keen on this evening—thus a number of raucous activities and superstitions have become associated with the holiday. Celebrated on hills or along the coast, these festivities often include sacrifices to holy springs, the plucking of magical herbs, and the construction of large bonfires, upon which are burnt effigies of witches and evil spirits. For a complete history of this holiday during the eighteenth and nineteenth centuries, see Eiler Nystrøm, *Offentlige Forlystelser i Frederik den Sjettes tid*, vol. 1 (Copenhagen: Gyldendalske Boghandel, 1913).

9. The Dyrehave comprises the grounds surrounding Ermitagen, a rococo palace belonging to the royal family. Located approximately fifteen miles north of Copenhagen in Klampenborg, this wooded area—originally the royal hunting grounds—was opened to the public by Frederik V in the mid-eighteenth century. Shortly thereafter an amusement park, Bakken, was opened on the grounds surrounding Kirsten Pil's Spring. To this day the Dyrehave serves as a favored retreat for Danes.

10. Adam Oehlenschläger, "St. Hansaftenspil," *Poetische Skrifter*, vol. 1 (Copenhagen: Det Nordisk Forlag, 1857), 3. "Velkommen i den røde Morgenstund / Enhver, som tidlig now har samlet sig, / For snart med ufortrodne, raske Fied / At folge os fra Byens dorske Taage / Til Skoven hist, som grøn og sval sig hvælver."

11. A figure originally from the Italian tradition of the *commedia dell'arte*, Harlequin became a popular theatrical character in early nineteenth-century Danish literature. Holberg was the first Dane to make use of the Harlequin figure, *De Usynlige*, and the Harlequin still appears in present-day performances of Casorti's Pantomime in Copenhagen's Tivoli. For a study of the Harlequin, see Otto Driesen, *Der Ursprung des Harlekins* (Berlin: A. Duncker, 1904).

12. For a discussion of Oehlenschläger's allusions to these figures, see Aage Kabell, "Sanct Hansaften-Spil," *Danske Studier* 76 (1981): 32–44.

13. Oehlenschläger, "St. Hansaftenspil," 7–8. "Nu er vi alle til Staden draget. / Stykkets Eenhed er just ei iagttaget; / Men de, som ei lide Changement, / Kan blive, naar vi flytte næste Gang. / Her er vi i Huus hos en Borgermand. / Men, Hillemænd! see, der kommer han. / Jeg faaer da vel at tage for Personen, / For ei at forstyrre Illusionen."

14. Ibid., 61. "Tryllende Harmonie / I midnatsdunkle Jord! / Salige Sympathie! / Hellige Poesie / Uden Ord! / Sammensmelting af Lund og Sø / Og Stierner og omsynget Yngling og Mø / Favn mod Favn / Tolker hele Naturen Kiærligheds Navn."

15. Discovered in 1583 by a maiden named Kirsten Pils, St. Kirsten's Spring (a.k.a Kirsten Pils' Spring or Brinkman's Spring) is a natural spring in the Dyrehave. This spring is often incorrectly referred to in popular literature as one of Denmark's "sacred" springs—i.e., a spring created through the miraculous actions of a saint. Little mention was made of the spring before the mid-eighteenth century, but in 1732 a dancer for the royal court named Brinkman re-discovered the spring and erected a small monument at its source. The spring is renowned for its healing qualities, and when Frederik V opened the Dyrehave to the general public, the spring became a popular attraction. According to legend, the medicinal powers of St. Kirsten's Spring are especially potent on St. Hans' Evening. To this day St. Kirsten's Spring is one of the Dyrehave's most popular attractions.

16. Oehlenschläger, "St. Hansaftenspil," 67. "I Maaneskin titter / Vi Fugle saa smaa / Bag Grenenes Gitter / Til hinanden, og slaae. / Gudskeelov, vi er ene / Paa vore smaae Grene! / Naar kun vi har Ro / Til at hoppe frit, / O, da er vi saa froe, / Saa froe, saa froe! / Quirilit, quirilit!"

17. In his sketches for the overture (DkB: Gade Saml. C II 6) Gade labels this horn passage "echo."

18. In *Agnete and the Merman* Gade uses a clarinet to represent Agnete. Likewise, a lone oboe presents "Selma's luscious tones" in the *Echoes of Ossian*.

19. DkB: Gade Saml. C II 6.

20. In 1838 he alluded to its "beauty" in a letter to A. P. Berggreen (see Harwell, "Gade's Early Compositions," 23–24).

21. According to Angul Hammerich, *Musikforeningens Historie 1836–1886* (Copenhagen: Musikforeningen, 1886), 84, Franz Glæser premiered the overture at a Music Society Concert in 1843.

22. According to Nils Schiørring, *Musikkens Historie i Danmark* (Copenhagen: Politikens Forlag, 1978), 2:303, *Alferne* was premiered in 1835 and soon became part of the Royal Theater's standard repertoire.

23. R. Larry Todd, *Mendelssohn: "The Hebrides" and Other Overtures* (Cambridge: Cambridge University Press, 1994), 53.

24. Ibid., 53–56.

25. For a thorough description of Mendelssohn's ingenious manipulation of motivic material in *A Midsummer Night's Dream* overture, see ibid., 54, 56–58.

26. Behrend, "Omkring Niels W. Gade," 67. The original letter is in the Helsted family's private collection. "Kjære Broder og Ven! ... Næst broderlig Hilsen og Salut melder jeg dig herved, at jeg befinder mig i bedste Velgaaende, frisk som en Fisk.... Jeg har lavet en nye ditto til Øhlenschlägers "St. Hansaftenspil" i A Dur som jeg vil lade opføre i Theatret ved en Koncert. Meget lystig og tillige erotisk (peent Stykke)."

27. Clara Schumann gave three concerts in Copenhagen—two at the Royal Theater (3 and 10 April) and a third at the Angleterre Hotel.

28. Berthold Litzmann, *Clara Schumann. Ein Künstlerleben. Nach Tagebüchern und Briefen* (Leipzig: Breitkopf und Härtel, 1910), 2:48. "Er [Gade] wird in meinem Konzert eine neue Ouverture von sich aufführen, die ganz verschieden von der ersten ist, sie ist ganz heiteren Charakters." The letter is dated 31 March 1842. Naturally Clara's mention of "der ersten" overture is a reference to the *Echoes of Ossian* overture, which Schumann would have known from the published four-hand arrangement (1841) and from performances in Leipzig by the Euterpe orchestra on 18 January 1842 (see K. W. W., *Der Musikverein Euterpe zu Leipzig 1824–1874. Ein Gedenkblatt* [Leipzig: C. F. Kahnt, 1874], 34) and the Gewandhaus orchestra on 5 February 1842.

29. *Fædrelandet*, 4 April 1842, 6724. "Publikum havde denne Aften Leilighed til at glæde sig ved et nyt Arbeide af den unge talentfulde Componist, Hr. Gade, en Ouverture til Øehlenschlägers 'St. Hans Aftenspil.' Denne Composition udmærkes sig ligesom hans forrige, ved smukke Ideer, Originalitet i Behandlingen og en prisværdig Forsmaaen af al Jagen efter ydre Effect, og erhvervede Componisten en varm og hædrende Anerkjendelse hos alle Musikkyndige."

30. *Det Berlingske Tidene*, 4 April 1842. "Blandt de andre Numere, hvoraf denne Concert bestod, maae vi især fremhæve vor talentfulde Capelmusicus N. W. Gades nye Ouverture til Oehlenschlägers 'Sanct Hans Aftenspil,' hvilken modtages med levende Bifald."

31. This manuscript is found in the Royal Library: Gade saml. C II 6. "Ouverture til Øhlenschlägers / 'St. Hansaftenspil' / (Op ?) (September 1841)."

32. See Dan Fog, *Musikhandel og nodetryk i Danmark efter 1750*, 2 vols. (Copenhagen: Dan Fog, 1984).

33. Especially appealing to mid-nineteenth-century Danish readers was Oehlenschläger's unprecedented use of a rich blend of literary genres. According to Hansen, "Adam Oehlenschläger and Ludwig Tieck," Oehlenschläger incorporated a wide variety of verse forms into his play, some of which were entirely new to Danish poetry (i.e., the Italian canzone and ottave). In the case of more traditional forms, Oehlenschläger often presented them in an unorthodox manner so as to produce a specific effect—for example blank verse in the vagabond's prologue, hexameter in

the highly satiric Idyll, and doggerel in the segment entitled "A man with a perspective case."

34. In fact, the first German translation of this work did not appear until 1853: *St. Johannis-Abend-Spiel. Dichtung von A. Oehlenschläger frei übergesetzt von Heinrich Smidt* (Berlin: Verlag von C. Grobe, 1853). As the title indicates, this edition of the play was a free translation. Consequently, many of the distinctive Danish characteristics in the original version were either omitted or altered considerably.

35. "Ouverture til Øhlenschlägers / 'St. Hansaftenspil' / (Op ?) (September 1841) / Kassert (?) / MUSICAL SIGNATURE / Skal 'Omarbeides.' "

36. "Oprindelig Ouverture til Øhlenschlägers / 'St. Hansaftenspil' / (Op ?) (September 1841) / Kassert (?) / MUSICAL SIGNATURE / Skal 'Omarbeides' / En Sommerdag / Idylleib Ouverture (1870)."

37. In 1886 Gade began work on a secular cantata entitled "St. Hans' Evening Play," but it was still incomplete at the time of his death. The composer Rued Immanuel Langgaard completed the orchestration for Gade's piece and added the hymn "Tryllende Harmoni." This revised version was published in Copenhagen in 1916 (*Sanct Hansaften Spil af Adam Oehlenschläger. Fragment af Slutningsscenen komponeret for Sopransolo, Kor og Orkester* [Copenhagen: Samfundet, 1916]).

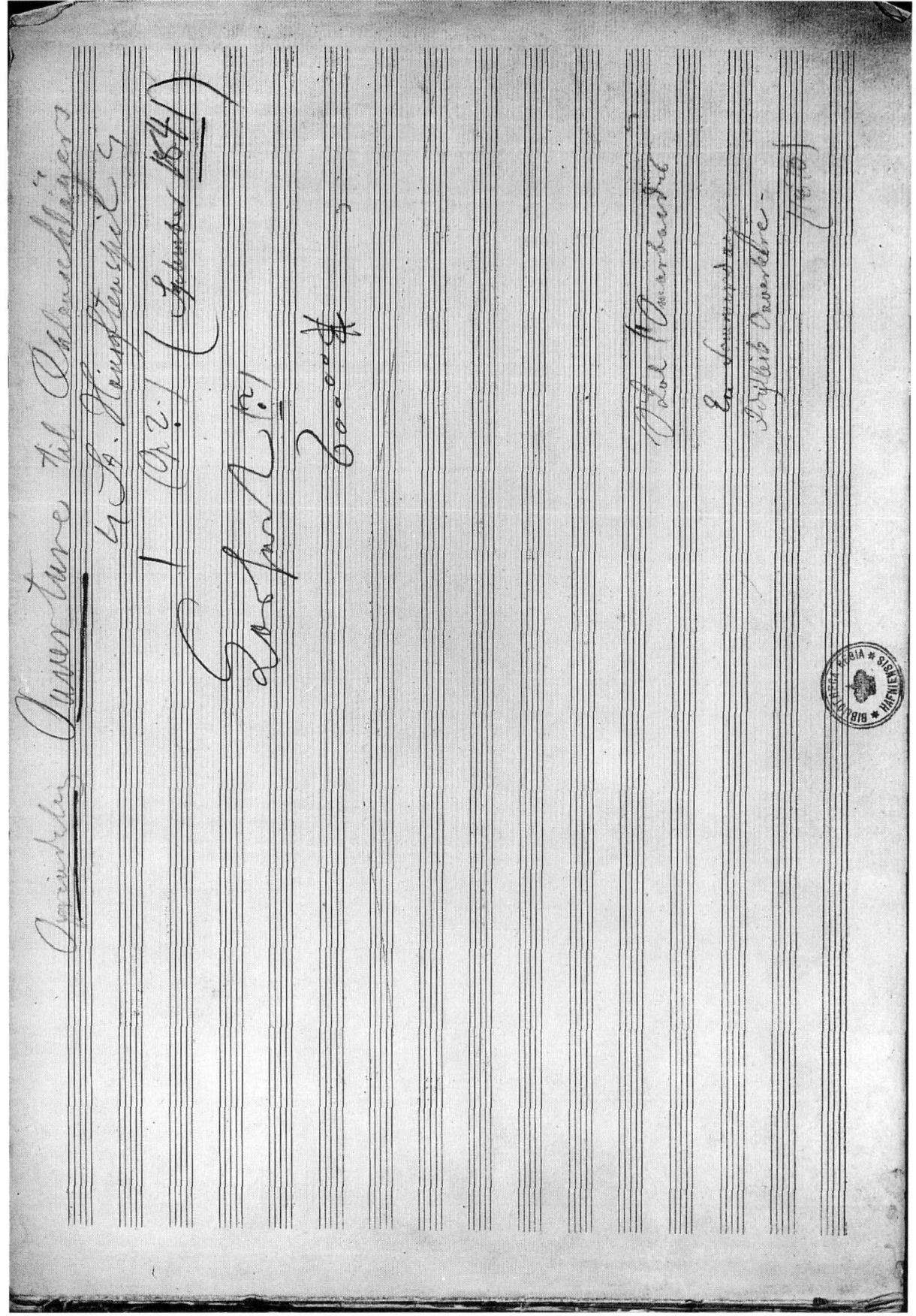

Plate 1. Niels W. Gade, *St. Hans' Evening Play Overture*, cover page of the autograph score. Courtesy of the Royal Library, Copenhagen.

Plate 2. Niels W. Gade, *St. Hans' Evening Play Overture*, beginning, page 2 of the autograph score. Courtesy of the Royal Library, Copenhagen.

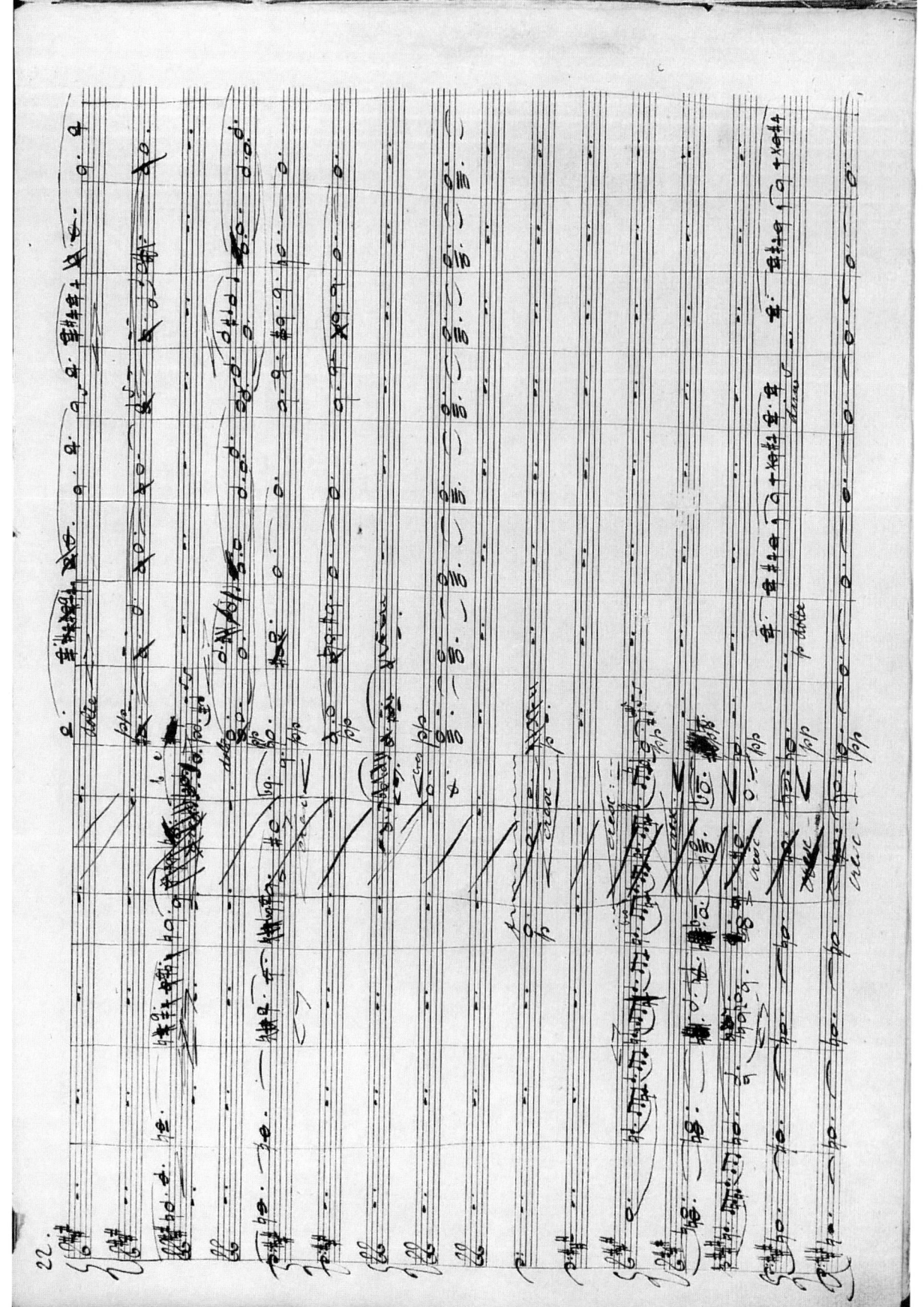

Plate 3. Niels W. Gade, *St. Hans' Evening Play Overture*, example of revisions made in 1870, page 22 of the autograph score. Courtesy of the Royal Library, Copenhagen.

St. Hans' Evening Play Overture

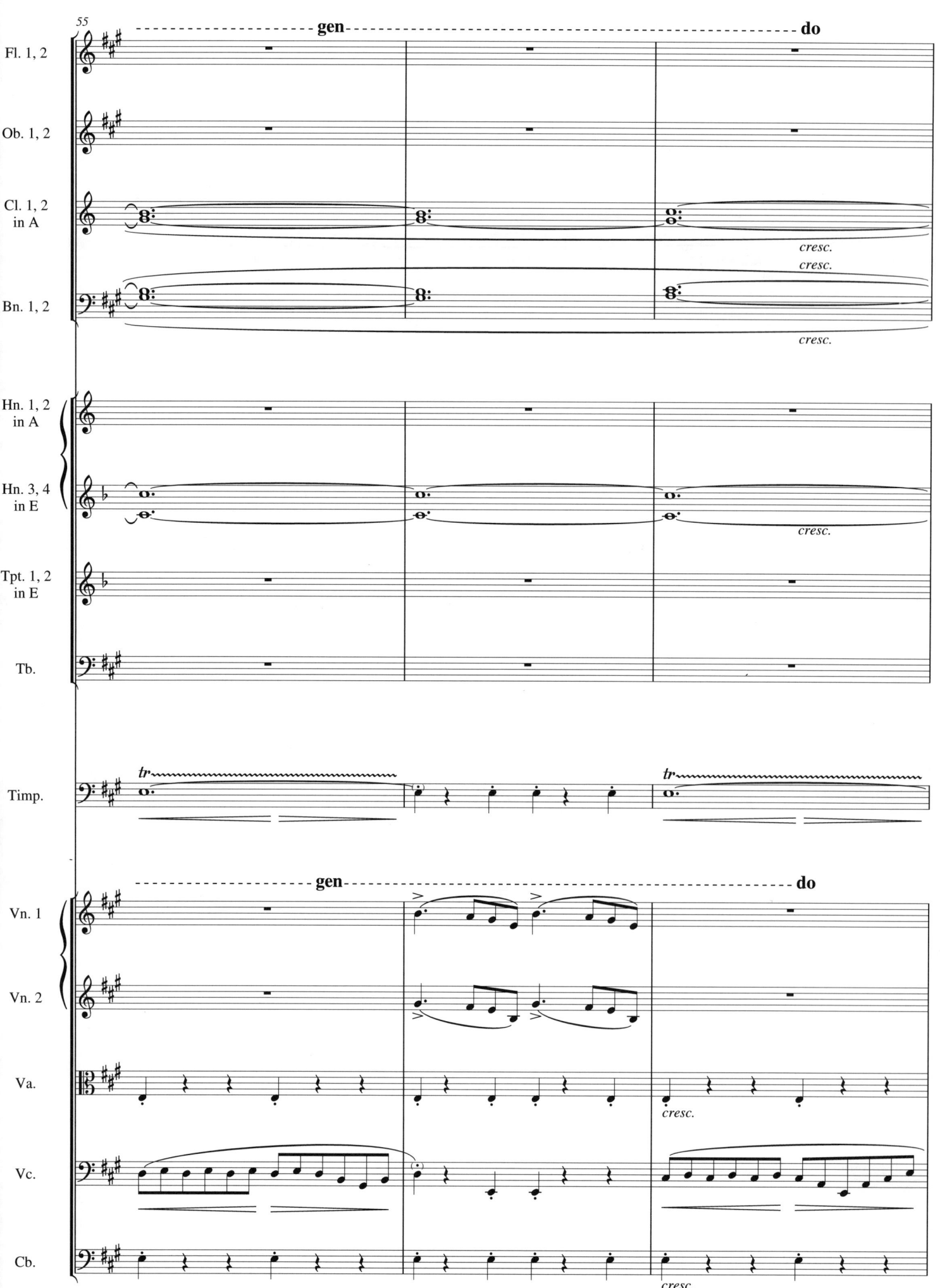

14

17

82
Fl. 1
Picc.
Ob. 1, 2
Cl. 1, 2
in A
Bn. 1, 2
Hn. 1, 2
in A
Hn. 3, 4
in E
Tpt. 1, 2
in E
Tb.
Timp.
Vn. 1
Vn. 2
Va.
Vc.
Cb.
sffz
mf
p
tr
2

85
Fl. 1
Picc.
Ob. 1, 2
Cl. 1, 2
in A
Bn. 1, 2
Hn. 1, 2
in A
Hn. 3, 4
in E
Tpt. 1, 2
in E
Tb.
Timp.
Vn. 1
Vn. 2
Va.
Vc.
Cb.
sffz
mf
tr
2
ff
p
fp

89
Fl. 1
Picc.
Ob. 1, 2
Cl. 1, 2
in A
Bn. 1, 2
a 2
Hn. 1, 2
in A
Hn. 3, 4
in E
Tpt. 1, 2
in E
Tb.
Timp.
Vn. 1
Vn. 2
Va.
Vc.
Cb.
tr
sffz
sfz
ff

21

22

23

24

105
Fl. 1
Picc.
Ob. 1, 2
Cl. 1, 2 in A
Bn. 1, 2
Hn. 1, 2 in A
Hn. 3, 4 in E
Tpt. 1, 2 in E
Tb.
Timp.
Vn. 1
Vn. 2
Va.
Vc.
Cb.

108
Fl. 1
Picc.
Ob. 1, 2
Cl. 1, 2
in A
Bn. 1, 2
Hn. 1, 2
in A
Hn. 3, 4
in E
Tpt. 1, 2
in E
Tb.
Timp.
Vn. 1
Vn. 2
Va.
Vc.
Cb.

27

115
Fl. 1
Picc.
Ob. 1, 2
Cl. 1, 2 in A
Bn. 1, 2
a 2
Hn. 1, 2 in A
Hn. 3, 4 in E
a 2
Tpt. 1, 2 in E
a 2
Tb.
Timp.
tr
Vn. 1
Vn. 2
Va.
Vc.
Cb.

29

124
C
1 solo
Cl. 1, 2
in A
dolce
Hn. 3, 4
in E
Vn. 1
pp
dolce
Vn. 2
pp
Va.
pp
Vc.
pp
Cb.
pp
130
Cl. 1, 2
in A
Vn. 1
Vn. 2
Va.
Vc.
Cb.

31

148
Fl. 1, 2
Ob. 1, 2
Cl. 1, 2
in A
1
Bn. 1, 2
Hn. 1, 2
in A
Hn. 3, 4
in E
Tpt. 1, 2
in E
Tb.
Timp.
Vn. 1
Vn. 2
Va.
Vc.
Cb.

33

158
1
Fl. 1, 2
Ob. 1, 2
Cl. 1, 2
in A
Bn. 1, 2
Hn. 1, 2
in A
Hn. 3, 4
in E
Tpt. 1, 2
in E
Tb.
Timp.
Vn. 1
Vn. 2
Va.
Vc.
Cb.

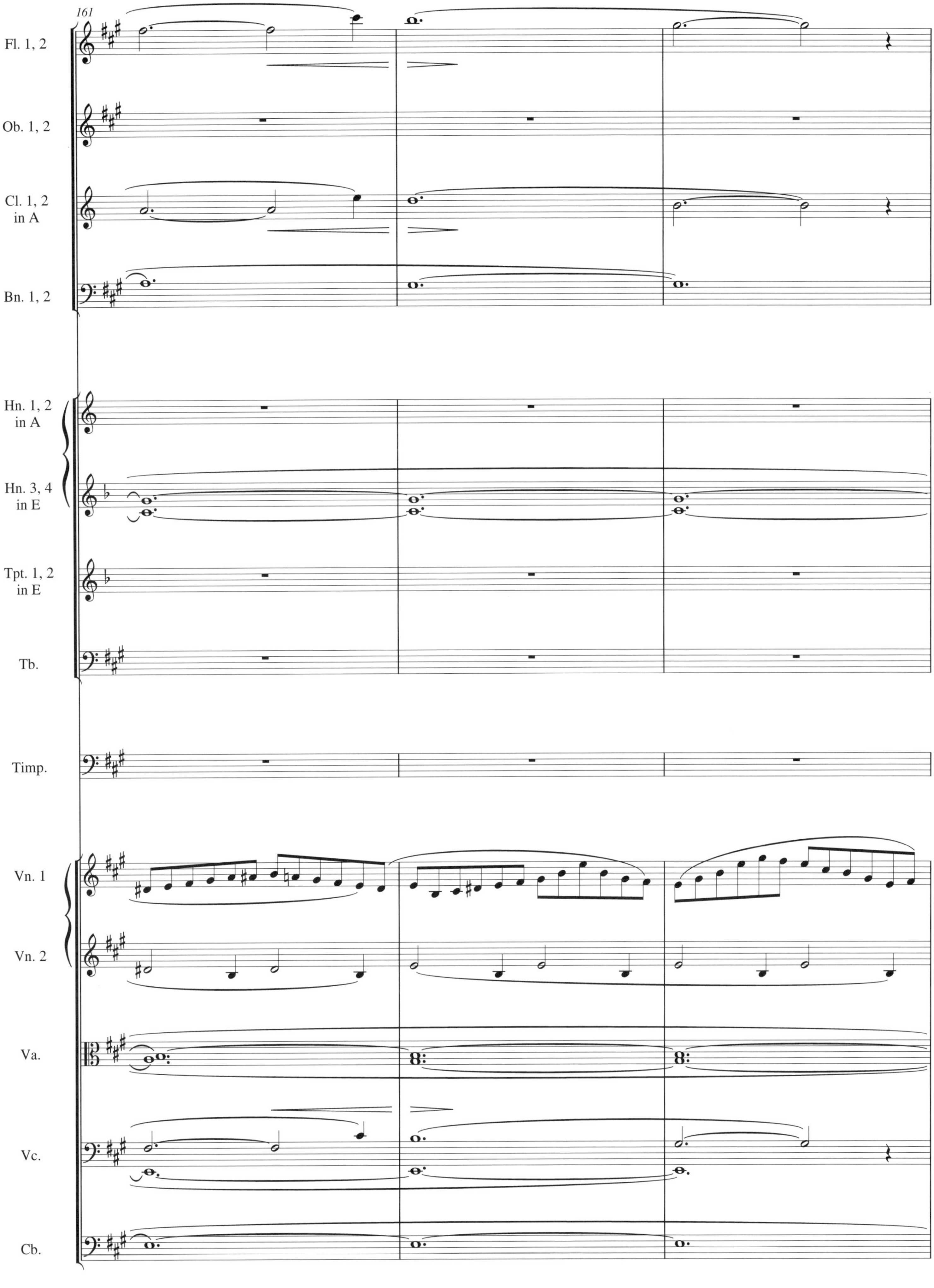
161
Fl. 1, 2
Ob. 1, 2
Cl. 1, 2
in A
Bn. 1, 2
Hn. 1, 2
in A
Hn. 3, 4
in E
Tpt. 1, 2
in E
Tb.
Timp.
Vn. 1
Vn. 2
Va.
Vc.
Cb.

36

37

38

39

176
Fl. 1, 2
Ob. 1, 2
Cl. 1, 2
in A
1
Bn. 1, 2
Hn. 1, 2
in A
p
Hn. 3, 4
in E
Tpt. 1, 2
in E
Tb.
Timp.
Vn. 1
p
Vn. 2
Va.
p
Vc.
Cb.

41

183
Fl. 1, 2
Ob. 1, 2
1
Cl. 1, 2
in A
Bn. 1, 2
solo
Hn. 1, 2
in A
cresc.
Hn. 3, 4
in E
Tpt. 1, 2
in E
Tb.
tr
Timp.
pp
cresc.
Vn. 1
Vn. 2
Va.
pp
cresc.
[tutti violoncelli]
arco
Vc.
pp
arco
Cb.
pp

43

191
Fl. 1, 2
Ob. 1, 2
Cl. 1, 2
in A
Bn. 1, 2
Hn. 1, 2
in A
Hn. 3, 4
in E
Tpt. 1, 2
in E
Tb.
Timp.
Vn. 1
Vn. 2
Va.
Vc.
Cb.
cresc.
tr
[cresc.
] mf

195
Fl. 1, 2
Ob. 1, 2
Cl. 1, 2
in A
Bn. 1, 2
a 2
Hn. 1, 2
in A
Hn. 3, 4
in E
Tpt. 1, 2
in E
Tb.
Timp.
Vn. 1
Vn. 2
Va.
Vc.
Cb.

199
Fl. 1, 2
Ob. 1, 2
1 solo
dolce
Cl. 1, 2
in A
dim.
Bn. 1, 2
Hn. 1, 2
in A
Hn. 3, 4
in E
Tpt. 1, 2
in E
Tb.
Timp.
Vn. 1
Vn. 2
Va.
Vc.
Cb.
[dim.]

47

48

49

218
Fl. 1, 2
Ob. 1, 2
Cl. 1, 2 in A
Bn. 1, 2
Hn. 1, 2 in A
Hn. 3, 4 in E
Tpt. 1, 2 in E
Tb.
Timp.
Vn. 1
Vn. 2
Va.
Vc.
Cb.
p
dim.
tr
pp
cresc.

223
Fl. 1, 2
Ob. 1, 2
Cl. 1, 2 in A
Bn. 1, 2
Hn. 1, 2 in A
cresc.
Hn. 3, 4 in E
in D
mute
Tpt. 1, 2 in E
Tb.
(tr)
tr
Timp.
cresc.
Vn. 1
Vn. 2
[trem.]
Va.
pp
cresc.
Vc.
cresc.
Cb.
cresc.

E
227
Fl. 1, 2
Ob. 1, 2
Cl. 1, 2 in A
Bn. 1, 2
Hn. 1, 2 in A
a 2
Hn. 3, 4 in E
a 2
Tpt. 1, 2 in D
a 2
Tb.
Timp.
(tr)
Vn. 1
Vn. 2
Va.
Vc.
Cb.

230
Fl. 1, 2
Ob. 1, 2
Cl. 1, 2
in A
Bn. 1, 2
Hn. 1, 2
in A
Hn. 3, 4
in E
Tpt. 1, 2
in D
Tb.
tr
Timp.
Vn. 1
Vn. 2
Va.
Vc.
Cb.

233
Fl. 1, 2
Ob. 1, 2
Cl. 1, 2 in A
Bn. 1, 2
Hn. 1, 2 in A
a 2
Hn. 3, 4 in E
a 2
Tpt. 1, 2 in D
Tb.
Timp.
Vn. 1
Vn. 2
Va.
Vc.
Cb.

236
Fl. 1, 2
Ob. 1, 2
Cl. 1, 2
in A
Bn. 1, 2
Hn. 1, 2
in A
Hn. 3, 4
in E
Tpt. 1, 2
in D
Tb.
Timp.
Vn. 1
Vn. 2
Va.
Vc.
Cb.

239
Fl. 1, 2
Ob. 1, 2
Cl. 1, 2
in A
Bn. 1, 2
Hn. 1, 2
in A
Hn. 3, 4
in E
Tpt. 1, 2
in D
Tb.
Timp.
Vn. 1
Vn. 2
Va.
Vc.
Cb.
a 2
sffz
mf
tr

57

247
Fl. 1
Fl. 2
Ob. 1, 2
Cl. 1, 2
in A
a 2
Bn. 1, 2
Hn. 1, 2
in A
Hn. 3, 4
in E
a 2
Tpt. 1, 2
in D
Tb.
Timp.
Vn. 1
Vn. 2
Va.
Vc.
Cb.
tr
ff
fp
p

251
Fl. 1
Fl. 2
Ob. 1, 2
Cl. 1, 2
in A
Bn. 1, 2
Hn. 1, 2
in A
Hn. 3, 4
in E
Tpt. 1, 2
in D
Tb.
Timp.
Vn. 1
Vn. 2
Va.
Vc.
Cb.
p
tr

254
Fl. 1
Fl. 2
Ob. 1, 2
Cl. 1, 2
in A
Bn. 1, 2
Hn. 1, 2
in A
Hn. 3, 4
in E
Tpt. 1, 2
in D
Tb.
Timp.
Vn. 1
Vn. 2
Va.
Vc.
Cb.
ff
f
sfz
sffz
a 2

F
258
Fl. 1
dim.
mf
p
Fl. 2
dim.
Ob. 1, 2
1 solo
dolce
Cl. 1, 2
in A
dim.
p
Bn. 1, 2
dim.
p
Hn. 1, 2
in A
Hn. 3, 4
in E
dim.
Tpt. 1, 2
in D
Tb.
Timp.
tr
pp
Vn. 1
dim.
p
pp
Vn. 2
dim.
p
pp
Va.
dim.
p
pp
Vc.
dim.
p
pp
Cb.
[dim.]
p
pp

262
Fl. 1, 2
Ob. 1, 2
Cl. 1, 2
in A
Bn. 1, 2
Hn. 1, 2
in A
Hn. 3, 4
in E
Tpt. 1, 2
in D
Tb.
Timp.
Vn. 1
Vn. 2
Va.
Vc.
Cb.
p dolce
dolce
tr
pp

63

269
Fl. 1, 2
Ob. 1, 2
Cl. 1, 2 in A
Bn. 1, 2
Hn. 1, 2 in A
Hn. 3, 4 in E
Tpt. 1, 2 in D
a 2
Tb.
Timp.
tr
Vn. 1
f
Vn. 2
sffz
Va.
Vc.
sffz
Cb.
sffz

272
Fl. 1, 2
Ob. 1, 2
Cl. 1, 2 in A
Bn. 1, 2
Hn. 1, 2 in A
Hn. 3, 4 in E
Tpt. 1, 2 in D
Tb.
Timp.
Vn. 1
Vn. 2
Va.
Vc.
Cb.
a 2
ff
fp
p

276
Fl. 1, 2
Ob. 1, 2
Cl. 1, 2 in A
Bn. 1, 2
Hn. 1, 2 in A
Hn. 3, 4 in E
Tpt. 1, 2 in D
Tb.
Timp.
Vn. 1
Vn. 2
Va.
Vc.
Cb.
a 2
ff
tr
cresc.
[cresc.]

67

68

285
Fl. 1, 2
Ob. 1, 2
Cl. 1, 2
in A
a 2
Bn. 1, 2
Hn. 1, 2
in A
Hn. 3, 4
in E
Tpt. 1, 2
in D
Tb.
Timp.
tr
Vn. 1
Vn. 2
Va.
Vc.
Cb.

G
288
a 2
Fl. 1, 2
sffz
p leggiero
Ob. 1, 2
1
Cl. 1, 2
in A
Bn. 1, 2
fpp
Hn. 1, 2
in A
Hn. 3, 4
in E
pp
3
Tpt. 1, 2
in D
Tb.
Timp.
p
Vn. 1
Vn. 2
Va.
Vc.
p dolce
Cb.
pizz.

291
a 2
a 2
Fl. 1, 2
Ob. 1, 2
Cl. 1, 2
in A
Bn. 1, 2
Hn. 1, 2
in A
Hn. 3, 4
in E
Tpt. 1, 2
in D
Tb.
Timp.
Vn. 1
Vn. 2
Va.
Vc.
pp
Cb.

72

297
a 2
a 2
Fl. 1, 2
Ob. 1, 2
Cl. 1, 2
in A
Bn. 1, 2
Hn. 1, 2
in A
Hn. 3, 4
in E
Tpt. 1, 2
in D
Tb.
Timp.
Vn. 1
Vn. 2
Va.
Vc.
Cb.

300
a 2
Fl. 1, 2
1
Ob. 1, 2
1
Cl. 1, 2
in A
Bn. 1, 2
Hn. 1, 2
in A
3
Hn. 3, 4
in E
Tpt. 1, 2
in D
Tb.
Timp.
Vn. 1
Vn. 2
Va.
Vc.
pp
Cb.

303
Fl. 1
Fl. 2
Ob. 1, 2
Cl. 1, 2
in A
Bn. 1, 2
a 2
Hn. 1, 2
in A
Hn. 3, 4
in E
Tpt. 1, 2
in D
a 2
Tb.
Timp.
tr
Vn. 1
Vn. 2
Va.
Vc.
Cb.
[arco]
ff

307
Fl. 1
Fl. 2
Ob. 1, 2
Cl. 1, 2
in A
Bn. 1, 2
a 2
Hn. 1, 2
in A
Hn. 3, 4
in E
a 2
Tpt. 1, 2
in D
a 2
Tb.
Timp.
tr
tr
tr
Vn. 1
Vn. 2
Va.
Vc.
Cb.

311
Fl. 1
Fl. 2
Ob. 1, 2
Cl. 1, 2
in A
Bn. 1
Bn. 2
Hn. 1, 2
in A
Hn. 3, 4
in E
Tpt. 1, 2
in D
a 2
Tb.
Timp.
tr
Vn. 1
Vn. 2
Va.
Vc.
Cb.
mf
p

78

319
Fl. 1
Fl. 2
Ob. 1, 2
Cl. 1, 2
in A
Bn. 1
Bn. 2
Hn. 1, 2
in A
Hn. 3, 4
in E
Tpt. 1, 2
in D
Tb.
Timp.
Vn. 1
Vn. 2
Va.
Vc.
Cb.
a 2
ff
tr

323
Fl. 1
mf
Fl. 2
Ob. 1, 2
1
mf
Cl. 1, 2
in A
dim.
Bn. 1
dim.
Bn. 2
dim.
a 2
Hn. 1, 2
in A
Hn. 3, 4
in E
a 2
Tpt. 1, 2
in D
Tb.
tr
Timp.
mf
Vn. 1
dim.
Vn. 2
dim.
Va.
dim.
tr
Vc.
dim.
Cb.
[dim.]

81

H
330
Fl. 1
dim.
p
Fl. 2
dim.
Ob. 1, 2
dim.
Cl. 1, 2
in A
dim.
p
Bn. 1
dim.
p
Bn. 2
dim.
p
Hn. 1, 2
in A
dim.
Hn. 3, 4
in E
dim.
p
Tpt. 1, 2
in D
a 2
Tb.
dim.
Timp.
Vn. 1
dim.
p
dim.
Vn. 2
dim.
p
dim.
pp
Va.
dim.
p
dim.
pp
Vc.
dim.
p
dim.
pp
Cb.
[dim.]
pp

83

84

85

366
Fl. 1, 2
1
dolce
Ob. 1, 2
Cl. 1, 2
in A
dim.
1
p
Bn. 1, 2
dim.
1
pp
Hn. 1, 2
in A
pp
Hn. 3, 4
in E
in D
Tpt. 1, 2
in D
Tb.
Timp.
Vn. 1
dim.
pp leggiero
Vn. 2
dim.
pp
Va.
dim.
pp
Vc.
solo
dim.
pp
[tutti]
Cb.
dim.
pp

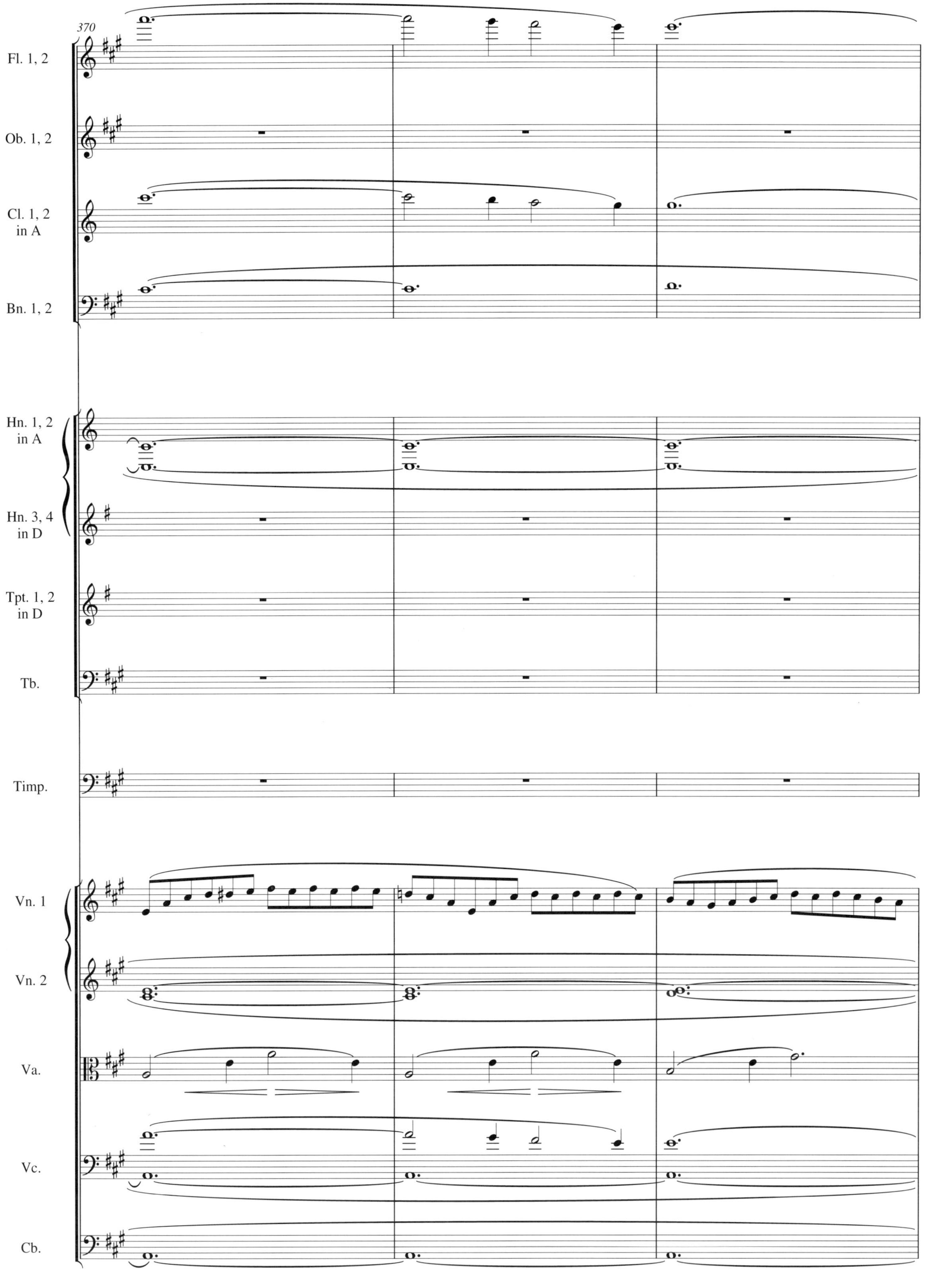
370
Fl. 1, 2
Ob. 1, 2
Cl. 1, 2
in A
Bn. 1, 2
Hn. 1, 2
in A
Hn. 3, 4
in D
Tpt. 1, 2
in D
Tb.
Timp.
Vn. 1
Vn. 2
Va.
Vc.
Cb.

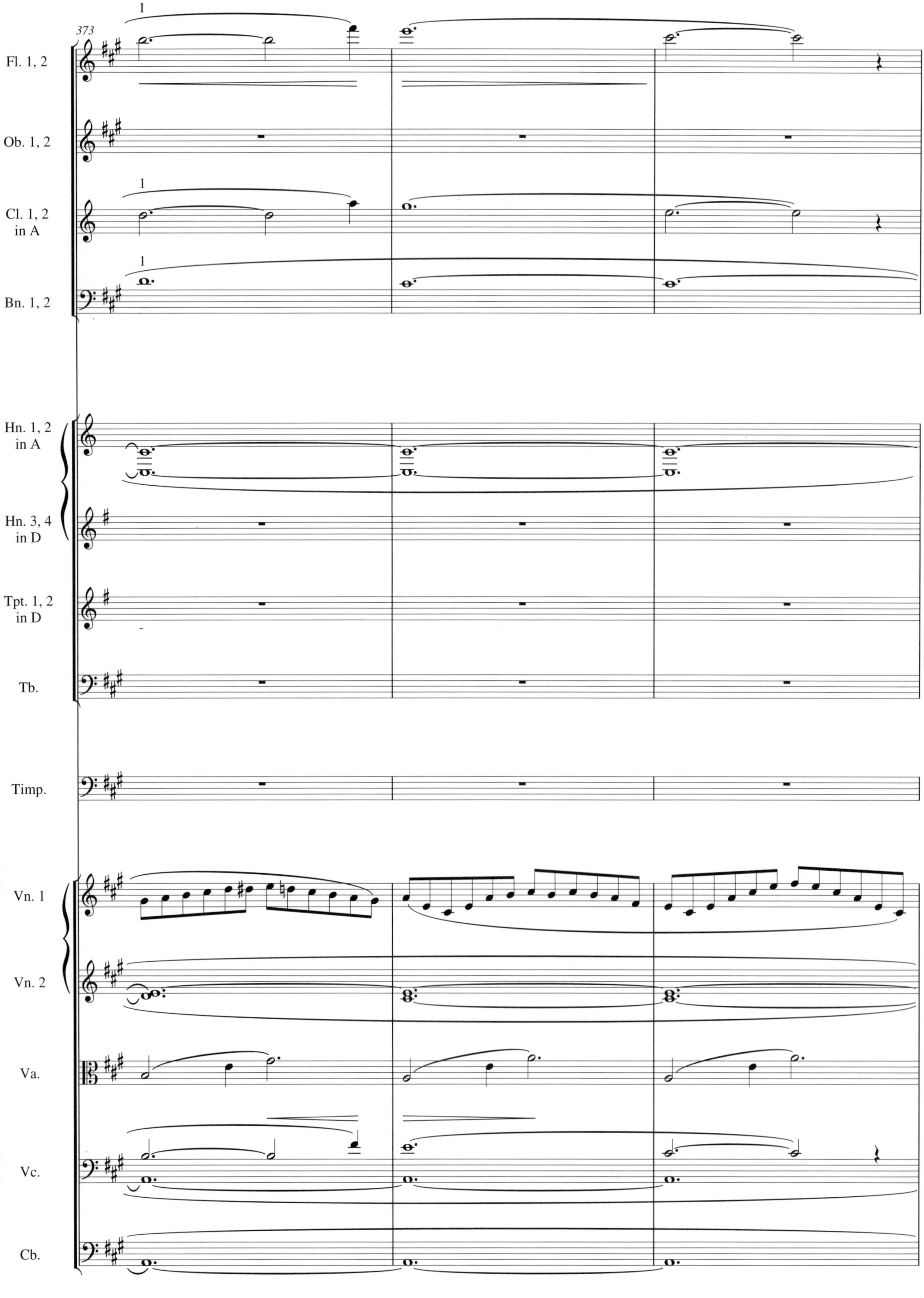
373
Fl. 1, 2
Ob. 1, 2
Cl. 1, 2
in A
Bn. 1, 2
Hn. 1, 2
in A
Hn. 3, 4
in D
Tpt. 1, 2
in D
Tb.
Timp.
Vn. 1
Vn. 2
Va.
Vc.
Cb.

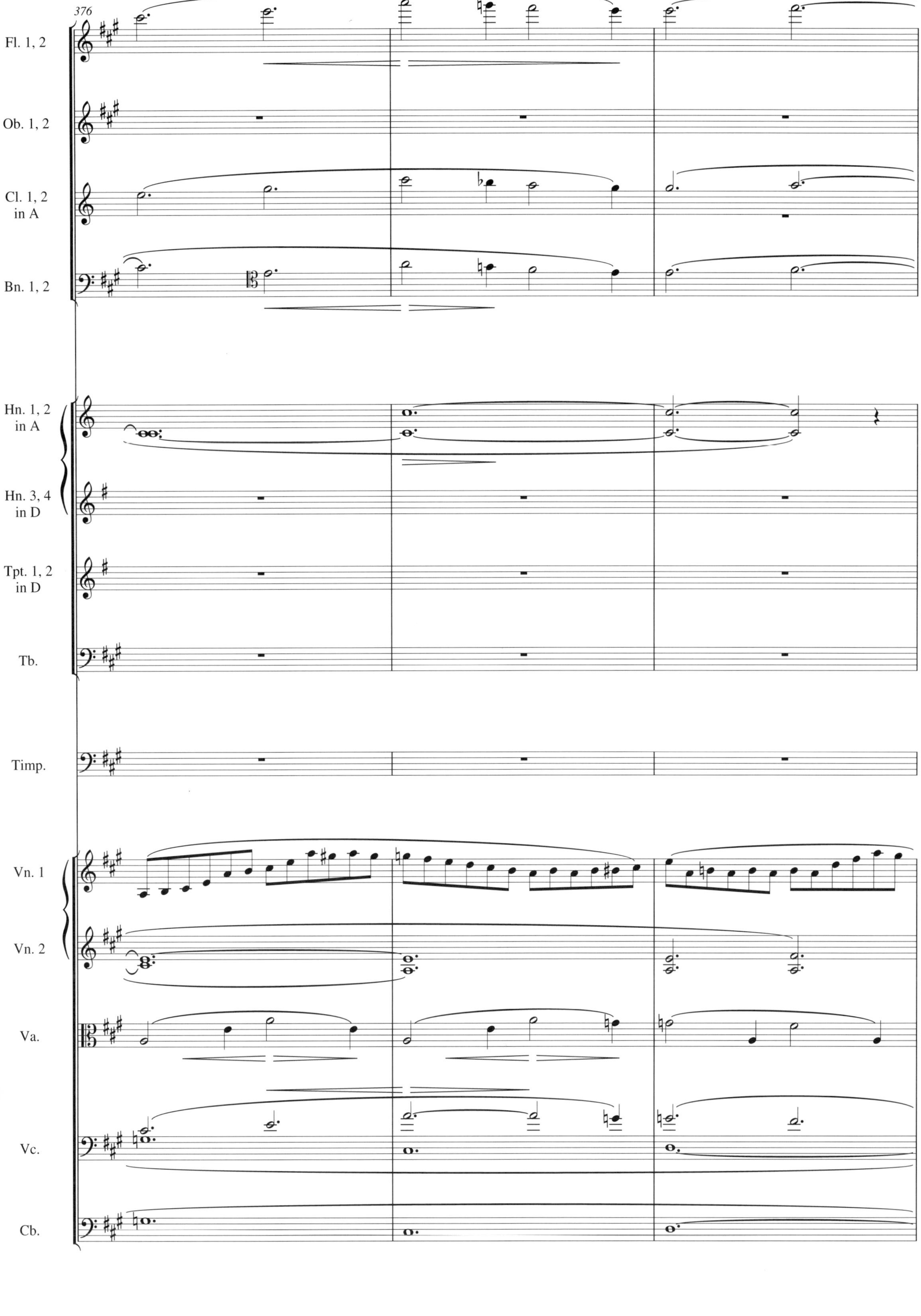
376
Fl. 1, 2
Ob. 1, 2
Cl. 1, 2
in A
Bn. 1, 2
Hn. 1, 2
in A
Hn. 3, 4
in D
Tpt. 1, 2
in D
Tb.
Timp.
Vn. 1
Vn. 2
Va.
Vc.
Cb.

379
1
Fl. 1, 2
Ob. 1, 2
Cl. 1, 2
in A
a 2
Bn. 1, 2
Hn. 1, 2
in A
p
Hn. 3, 4
in D
Tpt. 1, 2
in D
Tb.
tr
Timp.
pp
Vn. 1
Vn. 2
Va.
Vc.
Cb.

382
Fl. 1, 2
dim.
Ob. 1, 2
1
p
p
p
Cl. 1, 2
in A
sfz
sfz
p
p
Bn. 1, 2
p
sfz
p
Hn. 1, 2
in A
pp
Hn. 3, 4
in D
Tpt. 1, 2
in D
Tb.
tr
tr
Timp.
p
Vn. 1
p
Vn. 2
sfz
p
Va.
sfz
p
Vc.
sfz
p
Cb.
sfz
p

387
Fl. 1, 2
Ob. 1, 2
Cl. 1, 2
in A
Bn. 1, 2
Hn. 1, 2
in A
Hn. 3, 4
in D
Tpt. 1, 2
in D
Tb.
Timp.
Vn. 1
Vn. 2
Va.
Vc.
Cb.
p
dolce
dim.
sfz
pp
(tr)
[tutti violoncelli]

ritardando
poco
a
poco
393
Fl. 1, 2
dim.
Ob. 1, 2
1
p
pp
Cl. 1, 2
in A
dim.
pp
Bn. 1, 2
dim.
p
pp
1
pp
Hn. 1, 2
in A
dim.
p
a 2
pp
1
p
Hn. 3, 4
in D
Tpt. 1, 2
in D
Tb.
Timp.
tr
pp
ritardando
poco
a
poco
Vn. 1
pp
Vn. 2
p
pp
Va.
dim.
pp
Vc.
dim.
pp
Cb.
[dim.]
pp

400
Tempo primo
Fl. 1, 2
Ob. 1, 2
Cl. 1, 2
in A
1
Bn. 1, 2
1
1 solo
Hn. 1, 2
in A
p
Hn. 3, 4
in D
Tpt. 1, 2
in D
Tb.
(tr)
Timp.
Tempo primo
Vn. 1
Vn. 2
Va.
pp
[divisi]
Vc.
Cb.

406
Fl. 1, 2
Ob. 1, 2
Cl. 1, 2 in A
Bn. 1, 2
pp
pp
Hn. 1, 2 in A
Hn. 3, 4 in D
Tpt. 1, 2 in D
Tb.
Timp.
tr
pp
Vn. 1
Vn. 2
Va.
Vc.
Cb.

412
Fl. 1, 2
Ob. 1, 2
Cl. 1, 2
in A
Bn. 1, 2
Hn. 1, 2
in A
Hn. 3, 4
in D
Tpt. 1, 2
in D
Tb.
Timp.
Vn. 1
Vn. 2
Va.
Vc.
Cb.
mf
p
(tr)

418
Fl. 1, 2
1
dolce
Ob. 1, 2
Cl. 1, 2
in A
pp
Bn. 1, 2
1
Hn. 1, 2
in A
Hn. 3, 4
in D
Tpt. 1, 2
in D
Tb.
Timp.
Vn. 1
pp
Vn. 2
pp
Va.
pp
Vc.
pp
Cb.
pp

424
Fl. 1, 2
Ob. 1, 2
Cl. 1, 2
in A
Bn. 1, 2
Hn. 1, 2
in A
Hn. 3, 4
in D
Tpt. 1, 2
in D
Tb.
Timp.
Vn. 1
Vn. 2
Va.
Vc.
Cb.
1
pp
p con espressivo
p
dim.

430
Fl. 1, 2
dim.
Ob. 1, 2
Cl. 1, 2
in A
Bn. 1, 2
pp
Hn. 1, 2
in A
pp
Hn. 3, 4
in D
Tpt. 1, 2
in D
Tb.
Timp.
tr
pp
Vn. 1
ppp
Vn. 2
ppp
Va.
pp
dim.
ppp
Vc.
pp
dim.
ppp
Cb.
pp
[dim.]
ppp

436
Fl. 1, 2
Ob. 1, 2
Cl. 1, 2
in A
Bn. 1, 2
Hn. 1, 2
in A
Hn. 3, 4
in D
Tpt. 1, 2
in D
Tb.
Timp.
Vn. 1
Vn. 2
Va.
Vc.
Cb.
ritar
mute
(tr)
ppp

dan
do
442
Fl. 1, 2
1
pp
dim.
Ob. 1, 2
1
mf
con espressivo
dim.
Cl. 1, 2
in A
1
pp
dim.
Bn. 1, 2
pp
dim.
Hn. 1, 2
in A
Hn. 3, 4
in D
solo
pp
dim.
Tpt. 1, 2
in D
Tb.
Timp.
tr
dan
do
Vn. 1
pp
Vn. 2
pp
Va.
pp
Vc.
pp
Cb.

Critical Report

Sources

This edition presents the overture as it was performed on 3 April 1842 at the Royal Theater in Copenhagen. Only two sources appear to have survived for this overture: the autograph score used for the work's premiere and an earlier draft of the overture in piano format. Both sources are now held in the Royal Library in Copenhagen (DkB) in the Gade Collection (DkB: Gade Saml. C II 6). Gade's autograph served as the principal source for this edition.

Editorial Methods

The score order conforms with modern practice. Instrument names and abbreviations (originally in Italian) are given in English. Tempo and other written directives meant to apply to the entire score are placed above the top staff and above the first violins in the edition. The two treble clefs found in the source on staves meant for two instruments are reduced to one clef in the edition. The original keys of clarinets, horns, trumpets, and timpani are maintained but are stated in English ("in D," etc.). The notation of barlines and brackets follows modern conventions. Original note values are retained. The stem directions, beaming patterns, and rhythmic groupings of notes and rests in the source are made to conform with modern conventions in the edition.

The spelling, orthography, and placement of expressive and dynamic markings for individual parts (such as *dolce* and *cresc.*) are regularized. Any such added markings are placed in brackets; added ties and hairpins are dashed; added letter dynamics are set in bold (rather than the customary bold-italic) type. The source *ffz* is transcribed as *sffz*.

Articulations are regularized with respect to placement; those added (as called for by parallel passages, for instance) are placed in parentheses. The placement of slurs and ties is also regularized. Converging slurs (where one note marks the end of one slur as well as the beginning of another) are combined into a single slur unless doing so clearly disrupts the indicated phrasing. Where a slurred phrase includes tied notes, the slur is extended to encompass the tie.

For paired instruments sharing a single staff, common stemming is used where viable and where doing so does not diminish clarity. Opposing stemming is used wherever there are different note values and rest patterns between the two instruments. Voicing numerals and *a 2* designations found in the source are retained. Where these indications are added to express what is already expressed in the source by another means (as in specifying the upper part by notating it with upstems with rests for the lower part or in using double stems to indicate unison playing) they are not considered editorial and therefore are not bracketed. Voicing indications are repeated when an instrumental line continues over a page turn of the edition. The source uses separate staves for flute 1, flute 2 / piccolo, bassoon 1, and bassoon 2; where viable, the flutes and bassoons have each been combined on a single staff in the edition with the above policies implemented.

All editorially added accidentals are placed in brackets. Added cautionary accidentals are placed in parentheses; source cautionaries are retained only when they clarify passages. Accidentals of the source that are redundant by modern standards are tacitly removed. Key signatures have been added as required for the horns, trumpets, and timpani; accidentals thereby rendered redundant have been removed.

Critical Notes

The critical notes report all textual and musical differences between Gade's autograph score and this edition that are not otherwise covered by the stated editorial principles. Notes reporting changes made in preparing the edition are followed by notes reporting changes made by Gade in his revision of 1870. Locations within each piece are identified by measure number and then by instrument part name. Pitch names are standard: c' refers to middle C. The following abbreviations are used: M(m). = measure(s); Fl. = Flute; Picc. = Piccolo; Ob. = Oboe; Cl. = Clarinet; Bn. = Bassoon; Hn. = Horn; Tpt. = Trumpet; Tb. = Tuba; Timp. = Timpani; Vn. = Violin; Va. = Viola; Vc. = Violoncello; Cb. = Contrabass.

Notes on the Edition

M. 60, Hn. 2 has "mut: in A" (instruction on key moved to m. 44 in edition; on mute, to m. 62). Mm. 62–64, Bn. 2 lacks extension of slur. M. 66, Timp., Vn. 2, Va., Vc., Cb., *ff* at end of measure (moved to m. 67 in edition). M. 69, Bn. 2, note 2 has accent (moved to note 3 in edition). M. 78, Tb., note 2 is half note followed by one quarter rest. M. 99, Picc., note 1 has *mf*. M. 111, Hn. 3-4 has *cresc.* (changed to hairpin in edition). Mm. 140–41, Vc. has slur (extended back to begin with m. 139, note 2 in edition). M. 171, "Fl. traverso" indicates return to Fl. 2 (indication moved to m. 119 in edition). Mm. 185–86, Va. lacks crescendo dashing. M. 221, Tpt. 1-2 has "mut: in D" (instructions moved to m. 226 in edition). M. 232, Fl. 1, note 3 lacks crescendo hairpin. M. 239, Vc., bass clef returns as of note 1 (delayed until note 4 in edition). M. 247, Tpt. 1-2, chord 2 has staccato dot. M. 251 through m. 254, note 1, Bn. 1 is in tenor clef. M. 272, Hn. 3, note 2, ♮ sign has been added in the edition because of the editorial key signature. M. 273, Hn. 3, note 1, ♮ sign has been added in the edition because of the editorial key signature. M. 296, Cb. has *semp. pizz.* indication. Mm. 426 and 442, Ob. 1, instructions are "con expressivo" and "con exp.," respectively. M. 438, Hn. 3-4 has "mut: in D" (instruction on key moved to m. 368 in edition; on mute, to m. 441).

Notes on Gade's Revisions

M. 40, Hn. 1, note 1 changed to dotted whole note, note 2 and rest crossed out. M. 71, tempo changed to Allegro di molto; Ob. 1-2, chord 1 changed to half notes followed by quarter rests, ties crossed out, chord 2 changed to c♯' + a'. Mm. 71–75, Hn. 1-4, Tpt. 1-2, Timp., revised (see example 1). Mm. 71–76, Tb., each measure changed to dotted half note tied to half note plus quarter rest. M. 75, Ob. 1-2, chord 1 changed to half notes followed by quarter rests, chord 2 changed to d' + b'. M. 77, Tb., note 2 changed to half note. Mm. 77–78, Ob. 1-2, chord 2 changed to half notes. Mm. 77–82, Hn. 1-4, Tpt. 1-2, Timp., revised (see example 2). M. 83, Tpt. 1, note crossed out. M. 84, Bn. 2, all notation crossed out and

Example 1. Revisions in mm. 71–75

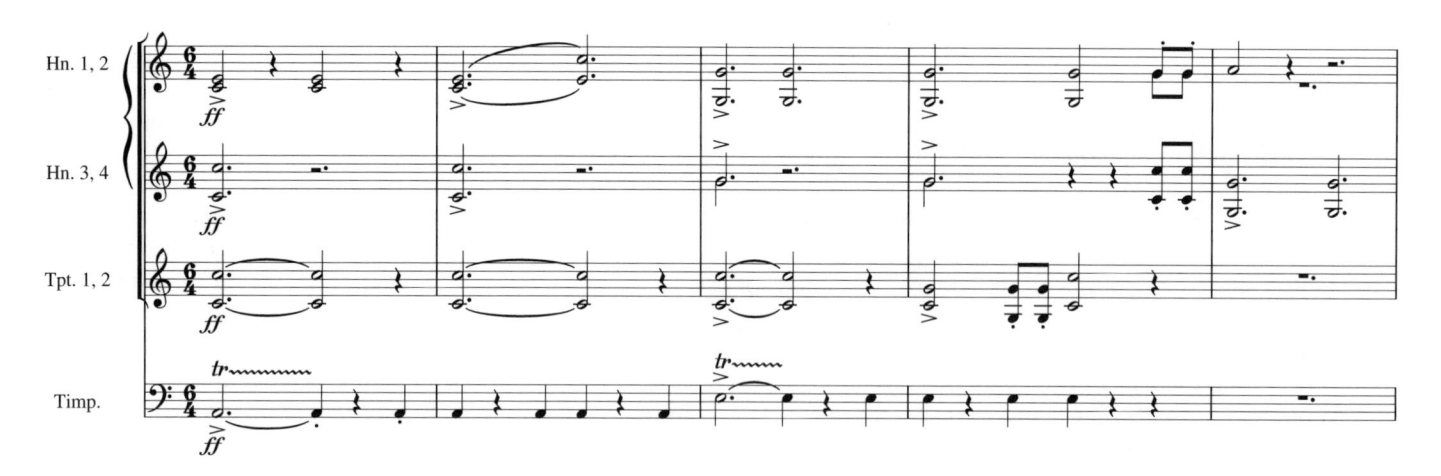

Example 2. Revisions in mm. 77–82

replaced with rest.   M. 84, Hn. 4, note crossed out and replaced with rest.   Mm. 84–89, Timp., revised:

M. 86 and m. 87 (first half), Bn. 2 and Hn. 4, notes crossed out and replaced with rests.   Mm. 86–89, Vc., revised:

M. 88, Bn. 2 and Hn. 4, note changed to quarter note followed by five beats of rests.   M. 89, Bn. 2 and Hn. 4, note 1 crossed out and replaced with rest.   M. 112, Ob. 1-2, chord 2 changed to c#′ + a′.   Mm. 112–15, Hn. 1-4 and Tpt. 1-2, revised:

Mm. 113 and 115, Timp., notation changed to quarter note A followed by quarter rest, two quarter note As, two quarter rests (all notes with staccatos).   Mm. 116–18, Ob. 1-2, music added:

Mm. 117 and 119, Tpt. 1-2, chord 2 crossed out and replaced with rest.   M. 127, Cl. 1, note 1 changed to dotted half note, note 2 crossed out, note 3 changed to dotted half note g″, note 4 crossed out.   M. 137, Cl. 1, note 1 changed to dotted half note g″ (replacing note 2).   M. 140, Vc., note 2 crossed out.   Mm. 141 and 143, Bn. 1 and Vc., note 1 crossed out.   M. 150, Cl. 1, note 1 changed to g″.   M. 151, Bn. 2, note 1, # crossed out. Mm. 151–53, Va., Vc., Cb., revised:

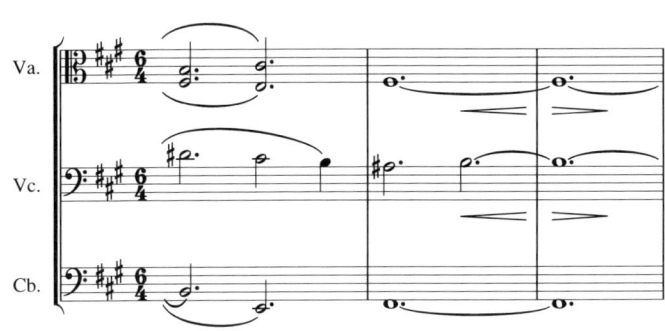

Mm. 153–55, Cl. 1-2, revised:

M. 154, Vn. 1 and Vn. 2, note 1 crossed out.   Mm. 154–55, Fl. 1-2, music added:

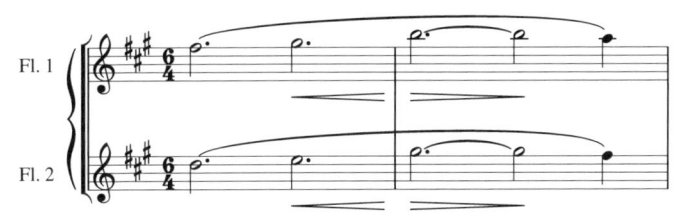

Mm. 156–63, all parts crossed out.   M. 164, Cb., note changed to e.   Mm. 164–70, Ob. 1, music added:

M. 165, Fl. 1, note 2 changed to b″, note 3 changed to a″, note 4 changed to g#″; Cl. 1, note 2 changed to d″, note 3 changed to c″, note 4 changed to b′.   M. 166, Fl. 1, note 1 changed to g#″; Cl. 1, note 1 changed to b′.   M. 175, Cl. 1, note 1 changed to dotted half note, note 2 crossed out, note 3 changed to d″, note 4 changed to b′; Vc. solo, note 1 changed to dotted half note, note 2 crossed out, note 3 changed to b, note 4 changed to g#.   M. 176, Cl. 1, note changed to c″; Vc. solo, note changed to a.   Mm. 179–81, Cl. 2 and Hn. 1, notes crossed out and replaced with rests.   M. 184, all parts crossed out.   M. 185, Cl. 1 has half note g″, Cl. 2 has half note g′, Bn. 1 has half note b, Bn. 2 has half note g (all notes tied from m. 183).   M. 185, Cb., *arco* begins on beat 4.   Mm. 185–92, Timp., revised:

Mm. 186–89, Fl. 1, music added:

Mm. 186–93, Cl. 1, music added:

M. 190, Fl. 1, note changed to c♮″. Mm. 190–93, Fl. 2, Ob. 1, Hn. 1, revised:

Mm. 195–98, Ob. 1-2, music revised:

M. 200, Bn. 1, note changed to dotted half note c♮′ followed by dotted half note d♮′; Bn. 2, note changed to dotted half note a followed by dotted half note b; Vn. 2, note changed to dotted half note c♮′ followed by dotted half note d′; Vc., notes crossed out and replaced with quarter note A slurred to half note g♮ followed by quarter note B slurred to half note g. M. 201, Bn. 2, note changed to quarter note c♮′ followed by five beats of rests. M. 203, Va., note changed to dotted half note followed by dotted half notes e + g. Mm. 204–6, Ob. 1, Bn. 1, Vn. 1, Vn. 2, Va., music revised:

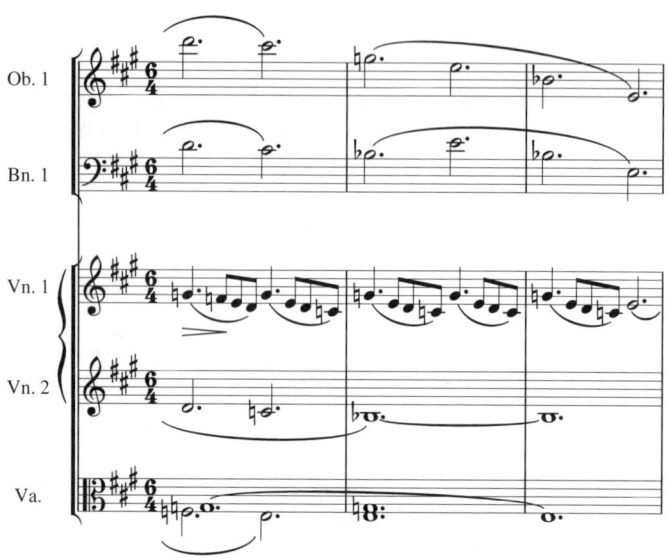

M. 205 (second half) and m. 206 (first half), all parts crossed out. Mm. 205–8, Hn. 1, revision added and then crossed out:

M. 207, Timp., all notation crossed out and replaced with rest; Vn. 1, note slurred to quarter note d♯′ followed by two quarter rests; Vn. 2, notes crossed out and replaced with dotted half note b♮. Mm. 207–15, Fl. 1-2, Ob. 1, Cl. 1-2, Bn. 1-2, revised (see example 3). Mm. 215–26, Vn. 1 and Vn. 2, music added (see example 4). M. 216, Hn. 1, added dotted half rest followed by dotted half note d″ with accent and *p*. M. 217, Ob. 1, added dotted half rest followed by dotted half note b″ with accent. M. 218, Hn. 1, added dotted half rest followed by dotted half note d″ with accent and slur to next measure. Mm. 224–26, Bn. 1-2, music added:

Example 3. Revisions in mm. 207–15

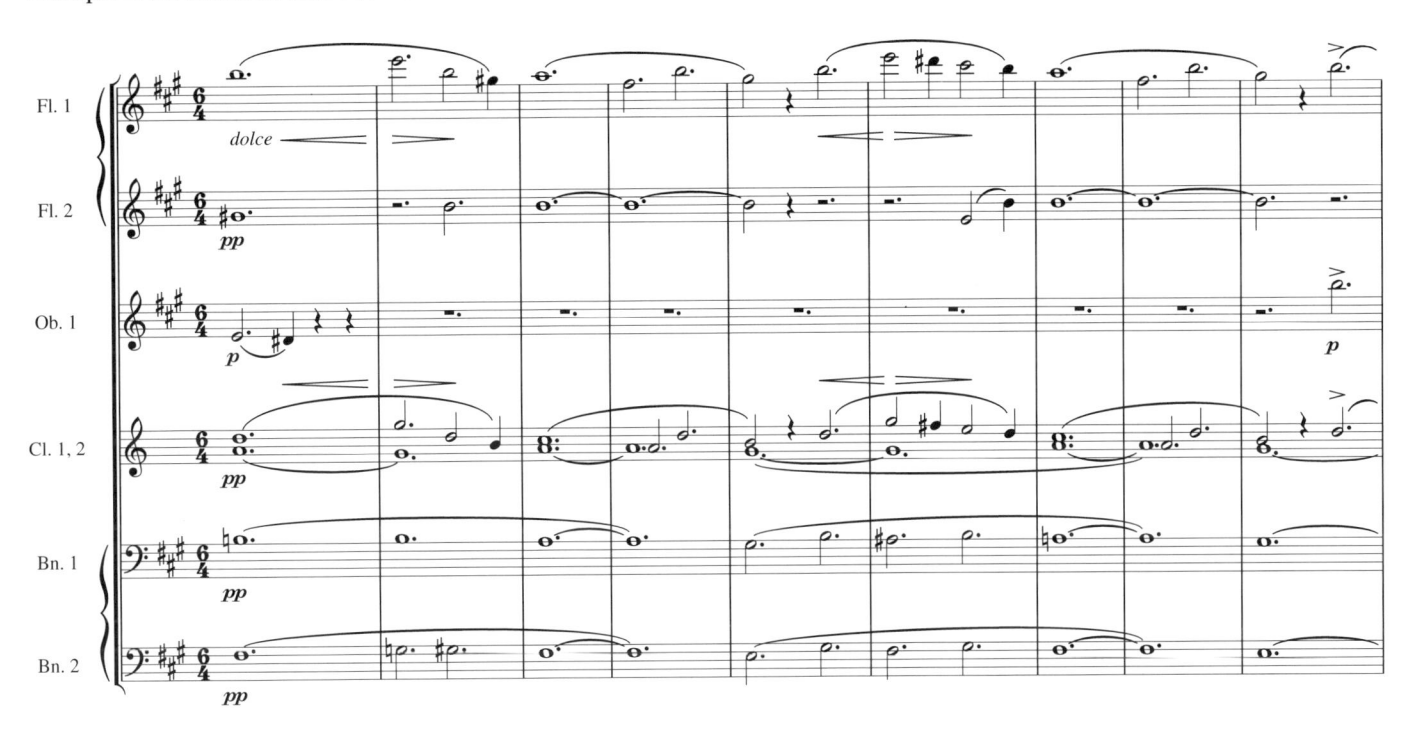

Example 4. Revisions in mm. 215–26

M. 240, Bn. 1-2, all notation crossed out and replaced with rests. M. 242 and m. 243 (first half), Bn. 1, notes crossed out and replaced with rests. M. 417, Fl. 1, added dotted whole note e''' with crescendo and decrescendo hairpins, *pp*, and slur to next measure (which equals m. 430; see next report). Mm. 418–29, all parts crossed out.

RECENT RESEARCHES IN THE MUSIC OF THE NINETEENTH AND
EARLY TWENTIETH CENTURIES
Rufus Hallmark, general editor

Vol.	Composer: Title
1–2	Jan Ladislav Dussek: *Selected Piano Works*
3–4	Johann Nepomuk Hummel: *Piano Concerto, Opus 113*
5	*One Hundred Years of Eichendorff Songs*
6	Etienne-Nicolas Méhul: *Symphony No. 1 in G Minor*
7–8	*Embellished Opera Arias*
9	*The Nineteenth-Century Piano Ballade: An Anthology*
10	*Famous Poets, Neglected Composers: Songs to Lyrics by Goethe, Heine, Mörike, and Others*
11	Charles-Marie Widor: *The Symphonies for Organ: Symphonie I*
12	Charles-Marie Widor: *The Symphonies for Organ: Symphonie II*
13	Charles-Marie Widor: *The Symphonies for Organ: Symphonie III*
14	Charles-Marie Widor: *The Symphonies for Organ: Symphonie IV*
15	Charles-Marie Widor: *The Symphonies for Organ: Symphonie V*
16	Charles-Marie Widor: *The Symphonies for Organ: Symphonie VI*
17	Charles-Marie Widor: *The Symphonies for Organ: Symphonie VII*
18	Charles-Marie Widor: *The Symphonies for Organ: Symphonie VIII*
19	Charles-Marie Widor: *The Symphonies for Organ: Symphonie gothique*
20	Charles-Marie Widor: *The Symphonies for Organ: Symphonie romane*
21	Archduke Rudolph of Austria: *Forty Variations on a Theme by Beethoven for Piano; Sonata in F Minor for Violin and Piano*
22	Fanny Hensel: *Songs for Pianoforte, 1836–1837*
23	*Anthology of Goethe Songs*
24	Walter Rabl: *Complete Instrumental Chamber Works*
25	Stefano Pavesi: *Dies irae concertato*
26	Franz Liszt: *St. Stanislaus: Scene 1, Two Polonaises, Scene 4*
27	George Frederick Pinto: *Three Sonatas for Pianoforte with Violin*
28	Felix Mendelssohn: *Concerto for Two Pianos and Orchestra in E Major (1823): Original Version of the First Movement*
29	Johann Nepomuk Hummel: *Mozart's* Haffner *and* Linz *Symphonies*
30–31	Gustav Mahler: *Die drei Pintos: Based on Sketches and Original Music of Carl Maria von Weber*
32	Niels W. Gade: *St. Hans' Evening Play Overture*